THE GHOSTLY TALES OF

OF

SLEEPY

HOLLOW

Published by Arcadia Children's Books
A Division of Arcadia Publishing
Charleston, SC
www.arcadiapublishing.com

Spooky America is a trademark of Arcadia Publishing, Inc.

First published 2021

ISBN 9781540247704

Library of Congress Control Number: 2021932534

Notice: The information in this book is true and complete to the best of our knowledge. It is offered without guarantee on the part of the author or Arcadia Publishing. The author and Arcadia Publishing disclaim all liability in connection with the use of this book.

Images courtesy of Shutterstock.com; p. 30 Brian Logan Photography/ Shutterstock.com.

THE
GHOSTLY TALES
OF
SLEEPY HOLLOW

JESSA DEAN

Adapted from *Legends and Lore of Sleepy Hollow and the Hudson Valley* by Jonathan Kruk

arcadia®
CHILDREN'S BOOKS

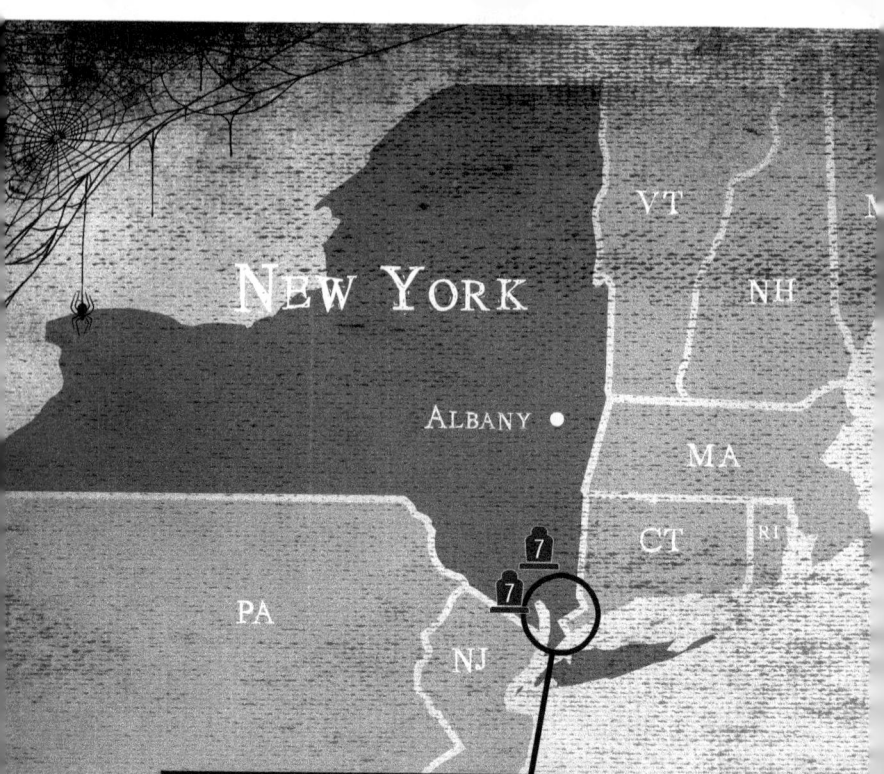

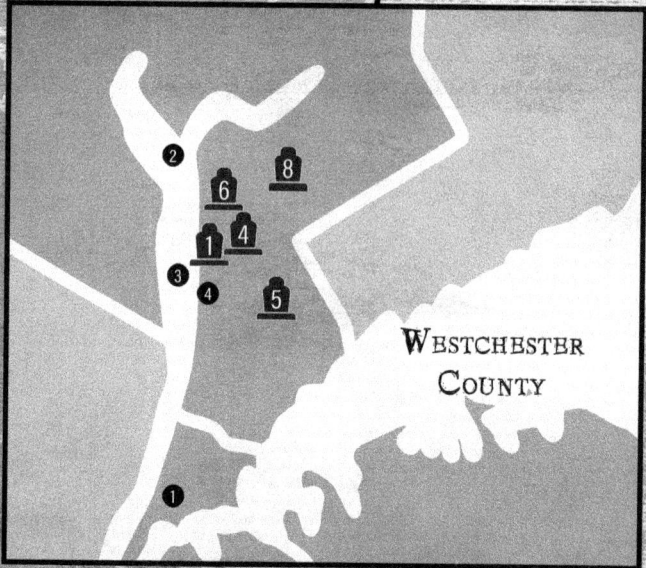

Table of Contents & Map Key

❶ Manhattan

❷ Hudson River

❸ Tappan Zee/Mario Cuomo Bridge

❹ Washington Irving's Sunnyside

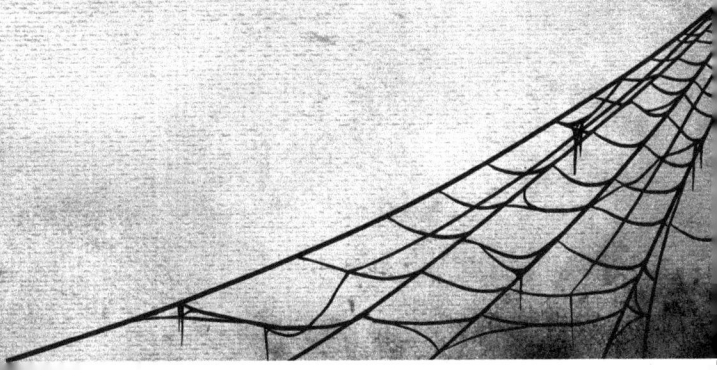

The Myths and Legends of Sleepy Hollow

Have you ever visited a place that felt like it didn't belong in our world? A place where the energy seemed to exist somewhere between the living and the dead?

Sleepy Hollow, New York, is that kind of place. In fact, the whole lower Hudson River Valley feels that way—like things aren't at all what they seem. The fog plays tricks with your mind. The wind moans and wails. You might even pass a few stone markers that look an awful lot like skulls. But if you like ghosts, Sleepy Hollow will excite you even as it scares you! Adding to the mystery is a ghostly tale that changed everything for the town of Sleepy Hollow. In fact, this tale blurred the line between fantasy and reality so much, no one truly knows where one ends and the other begins.

You can't talk about the lower Hudson River Valley—especially the haunted parts—without talking about "The Legend of Sleepy Hollow," written in 1820 by Washington Irving. Irving wrote his ghostly tale so well that people assume it actually happened. Why else would he have called it "The Legend of Sleepy Hollow?" The "Legend" mixes real places and people with local and traditional folklore to create a story that thrills and scares readers just as much today as it did when it was published. Today, it's required reading in many schools, and there are many movies and books that have adapted the tale. Thousands of tourists flock to Sleepy Hollow each year, especially during Halloween, to visit the places mentioned in the story.

Reading Irving's "Legend" pulls you so much into a spooky atmosphere that it's hard to believe he wasn't in New York when he wrote it. He lived in Birmingham, England, at the time, but he loved Sleepy Hollow and the surrounding areas so much that he eventually settled nearby.

Washington Irving

You can visit his home, called Sunnyside, but you might be confused about how to actually get there. Some claim it's in Irvington, which was named after the author himself, while

others say it's in Tarrytown, which was the town established first, just three miles north of Irvington. This just goes to show you how much Irving and his "Legend" are loved in the region.

But that's not even the coolest thing about Irving's connection to Sleepy Hollow, because Sleepy Hollow technically didn't even exist until Irving created it! It was known as North Tarrytown until 1996. That year, the main employer in North Tarrytown—an automobile plant—shut down. Without the jobs it provided, the town would have really become a "ghost town" of empty houses and buildings as people moved away. However, local leaders had a brilliant idea to save their town.

Everyone already believed Irving's tale: they came to North Tarrytown from near and far to chase ghosts. So the town decided to become the one Washington Irving created. Instead of manufacturing cars, the town changed its name to Sleepy Hollow and transformed into a major tourist destination for those who seek out the supernatural. (Don't worry; going forward, we'll always refer to the town as Sleepy Hollow to avoid confusion.)

No one can deny the area draws to it all things spooky, including people who love to chase the things that go bump in the night. In fact, long before Washington Irving spun his tale, it was rumored that ghosts walked freely among the hills and fields of the lower Hudson River Valley.

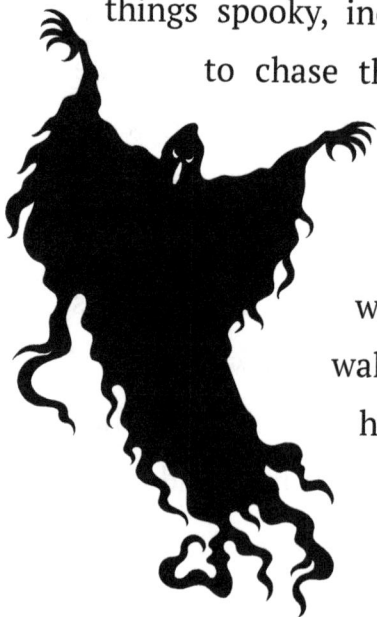

The indigenous tribes of the area told stories of supernatural things and tribe members who had been killed while protecting their territories. The Revolutionary War brought more bloodshed to the region. With such a history of struggle, it's no wonder the streets of Sleepy Hollow possess a particular kind of haunted energy. It's almost as though a spell has been cast on the town. Frightened residents report seeing strange things and hearing odd music and loud, lonesome cries floating through the air. They see shapes in the mist and figures high in the hills.

But was Sleepy Hollow actually the home of a Headless Horseman, as described in Irving's tale, who chased local people for their heads?

The answer? Anything seems possible in Sleepy Hollow.

Will you encounter a ghost if you walk its pathways alone under the darkness of night? There's a good chance of it.

So, if you really want to know more about this truly spooky part of America and the

legends that locals tell, read on. But be warned! The Headless Horseman isn't the scariest thing lurking near the banks of the Hudson River. It's quite possible you'll find something even more unsettling to haunt your dreams!

Ichabod's Tale

For those who haven't read "The Legend of Sleepy Hollow," the story features Ichabod Crane, a traveling schoolteacher from Connecticut who wandered into Sleepy Hollow and never made it out. Or did he?

Ichabod was a peculiar character. He looked like a scarecrow who'd come to life and jumped off his post in the cornfield. His beak-like nose and long, skinny arms and legs seemed perfect for someone named after a bird. During the day, Ichabod was a strict schoolteacher. He didn't let the kids get away with anything in class. And they couldn't get away from him. At night, he stayed with them, spending a few weeks at a time in a different student's home instead of having his own place. Can you imagine having your mean teacher sit across from you at dinner every night? But kids whose parents weren't good cooks didn't have to worry about this unwanted visitor. Ichabod made sure to seek out only the best cooks in Sleepy Hollow!

Quickly, Ichabod became known around town for two things: being picky about food and being obsessed with gross, spooky tales. He wanted to hear all the legends and lore of Sleepy Hollow, even the most gruesome, bloody ones that people didn't want to talk about. Nothing was too much for Ichabod, and Sleepy

Hollow had many tales to tell! Creepy houses, cursed streams, and haunted barns filled the area. Many people claimed that ghosts haunted the streets of Sleepy Hollow and wailed from high above the river, warning of storms to come. Ichabod took it all in, grinning and giggling and calling for more. Never mind the real people affected by the tales; Ichabod couldn't get enough.

However, one tale stole his attention above all others: the Headless Horseman.

The townspeople feared the Horseman more than anything in the world. This former soldier had lost his head on the battlefield

when a cannonball took it right off. That left a ghoul searching to replace what had been taken from him. At night, they heard his horse galloping and snorting outside. No one wanted to be caught out late at night when the Horseman prowled the streets.

But as fascinated as Ichabod was with the dead who wandered Sleepy Hollow, he was equally obsessed with one of the living. Katrina van Tassel caught Ichabod's eye immediately. He wasn't alone. Many men in Sleepy Hollow hoped to marry the beautiful Katrina. It didn't hurt that her father, Baltus, owned half the town.

Ichabod looked at the van Tassels' wheat fields and fruit orchards and imagined the day they would all be his. He thought spending time with Katrina as her singing instructor would be enough to win her over and make his dreams of wealth come true. But he had competition in a man named Brom Bones, who was tall and muscular—the physical opposite of Ichabod.

Brom didn't like Ichabod interfering with the love of his life, so he pulled all kinds of pranks, hoping to get Ichabod to move to another town. He tried pumping smoke into the schoolhouse. He set booby traps to annoy and distract Ichabod. He even trained a dog to howl whenever Ichabod gave singing lessons to Katrina! It was enough to drive anyone to the next town, but Ichabod wouldn't leave.

Finally, Brom saw a chance to get rid of his rival for good.

The van Tassel family held an annual fall party, and Ichabod arrived in style. He dressed in his best suit, slicked his hair back, and borrowed a grumpy old horse named Gunpowder to ride to the van Tassel farm. He patted his pocket, which contained a love poem he planned to give Katrina after the party. Surely that would make her say yes if he asked her to marry him.

As Ichabod entered the van Tassel land, he again imagined having all of it to himself. He pictured living there on the massive farm in that beautiful house, walking the fields in the sun, and sitting down to fancy dinners at the table. He wanted it more than anything. At the party, Ichabod ate piles of rich food and then jumped onto the dance floor when a violin began to play. He swung Katrina around the dance floor as the entire party cheered them on. All except for Brom, that is.

Brom had been plotting his scheme to rid the town of Ichabod for good, and when the music stopped, he went right to work. He convinced the old veterans to start talking about the Revolution and the bloody battles they fought. Of course, that led to the tales of the ghosts of Sleepy Hollow and the spirits of those who died on the battlefields. Then, just as Brom hoped it would, talk turned to the tale of Farmer Brouwer, an old Sleepy Hollow resident who denied any belief in ghosts. Unfortunately for Brouwer, though, he fell victim to the Headless Horseman. One fateful evening, the Horseman disappeared into darkness with the poor farmer's head! Brom followed that up with his own story of racing the Headless Horseman across the bridge to safety as the ghoul vanished in a flash of fire. "You see," Brom said to a shocked Ichabod, "he cannot cross the bridge by the Old Dutch Church graveyard."

Not long after that, Baltus van Tassel broke up the party. Ichabod sought out Katrina to declare his love, but she sent him away. Rejected and sad, Ichabod returned to Gunpowder and headed home. As he rode, the night began to play tricks on him. As the stories he'd heard played over and over in his mind, he began to see danger lurking in every shadow, ghosts behind every tree. Each creak or groan sent his heart racing, and stubborn Gunpowder wouldn't move faster.

Then Ichabod clearly heard someone else on the road. He called out, "Who are you?" but got no answer. He finally spotted his fellow traveler against the night sky. The rider sat tall in the saddle and wore a flowing cloak, making him look even larger. Already spooked, Ichabod's veins turned to ice when he saw the body had no head. Instead, the head rested on the top of the horse's saddle.

Brom's words echoed in Ichabod's brain. "If I can just make it to that bridge," Ichabod thought, "the Headless Horseman cannot cross!" He squeezed Gunpowder so hard that he broke the saddle. The horse's hooves pounded as loud as Ichabod's heart as he rode for the bridge. He reached it first and then looked back. There the Horseman stood, rotted head in hand, and hurled it at Ichabod, striking him in the head.

The next morning, Gunpowder's owner found him grazing nearby, with Ichabod nowhere to be found. Without their schoolteacher, the kids got a holiday. But what became of Ichabod? Nobody knew.

Later on, the townspeople made a frightening discovery under the bridge: the remains of Ichabod's brain right next to the love poem he'd written for Katrina. A few locals said the mess was pumpkin mash, not brains, but no one listened. Ichabod was never seen again. The farm wives who know the legends of Sleepy Hollow insisted the Headless Horseman sent Ichabod to his grave that night, convinced they could still hear his ghostly singing where his schoolhouse once stood.

CHAPTER 3

The Story Behind the Story

Washington Irving did use a lot from Sleepy Hollow history to make his tale feel real to the reader. Places were only lightly disguised. He used names of real townspeople to represent his fictional characters. He also blended stories from soldiers and sailors, myth and legend from other countries, to bring a dose of the real world into his ghostly tale. In fact, many fans of the "Legend" don't know that Ichabod Crane was a real person.

Irving stole the name from an Army major he knew through friends. The real Ichabod disliked that Irving used his name without permission, but the name was the only similarity between our favorite fictional schoolteacher and this particular serviceman. In fact, "Ichabod" wasn't actually that unusual of a name back then.

The thing that drew most readers into Irving's story was fear. Locals at the time never forgot the particularly ruthless soldiers who fought for the British in the Revolutionary War. They were called Hessians, and they were German soldiers who trained for war starting at age seven. Can you imagine training for war instead of going to school? Some Hessians were ready for combat—meaning they could go to

war—at just sixteen years old!
Hessians were taught to be
violent and merciless. Many
American fighters during
the Revolution had few
supplies and had never
been in battle before.
They were no match
for the Hessians. Many
Americans would drop
their weapons and run
when they saw Hessians
coming. Even decorated
soldiers couldn't bear to
face these warriors.

Rumors spread throughout the colonies
about the power and cruelty of the Hessians.
They towered over everyone with piercing
eyes, had razor-sharp mustaches, and could be

spotted from far away because of their miter caps—custom helmets made of strong pieces of brass, each with a fierce lion carved into the front and a chin strap to keep it in place. Some people spotted the Hessians at a distance and confused the chin straps and mustaches for two sets of teeth! This led to even more rumors— of cannibalism. They weren't true, of course, but the colonists were afraid that the Hessians would eat their children if they were caught.

Picture these monstrous warriors coming down the road toward the colonists, their gold helmets glinting in the sun and empty bellies hungry for flesh. Maybe now you can understand why the colonists had such a hard time forgetting the Hessians. Many must have had nightmares long after the Revolutionary War, especially if they had served in combat, as the Revolution ended in 1783—only thirty-seven years before "The Legend of Sleepy Hollow" was written. Terror was fresh in the colonists' minds. Irving knew that focusing on the tales of the Hessian warriors would keep readers' attention. When the villain of Irving's story was revealed to be a supernatural soldier, people's past experiences and fears became a strange mix of fact and fiction. It was as though they felt the presence of evil lurking around every corner, just like *you* might expect to feel after reading the "Legend." Only for the colonists, they had already looked into the eyes of the beast, so it was too easy for them to believe the undead were coming for them.

Old Dutch Church of Sleepy Hollow

The Birth of a Legend

Writing is a little like magic. A writer can take bits and pieces of inspiration, ask questions and seek answers at the same time, and then turn something totally familiar into something completely new. But there's always a sense of something unexplainable, some kind of supernatural luck that pulls a story together. For Washington Irving, the town of Sleepy Hollow *was* the unexplainable magic. It's fair to say that the town put him under a supernatural spell of its own. But the road to creating "The Legend of Sleepy Hollow" didn't begin in New York. It actually started in London.

One Sunday morning in 1818, at the age of thirty-five, Washington Irving and his brother Peter walked through the fog that rolled onshore from the River Thames. Soon they heard the ringing of the bells from St. Martyr's Church, but instead of running off to services, Washington stopped in his tracks, with the fog surrounding him. He was certain he saw a figure forming in the mist from out of the corner of his eye, startling him to his core. He asked Peter if he had seen the shape as well, but Peter—mentioning the bell and being late for church—teased Washington about seeing a headless rider on horseback. Nonetheless, Irving couldn't let go of the image he believed he saw, so he left Peter to attend church alone and ran home to write about it. While versions of this story have been told many times throughout the years, biographers generally agree that something about Irving's time in London inspired him to write "The Legend of Sleepy Hollow."

Irving was born in Manhattan in 1783. Most of his friends were Dutch, and he would sneak off with them to

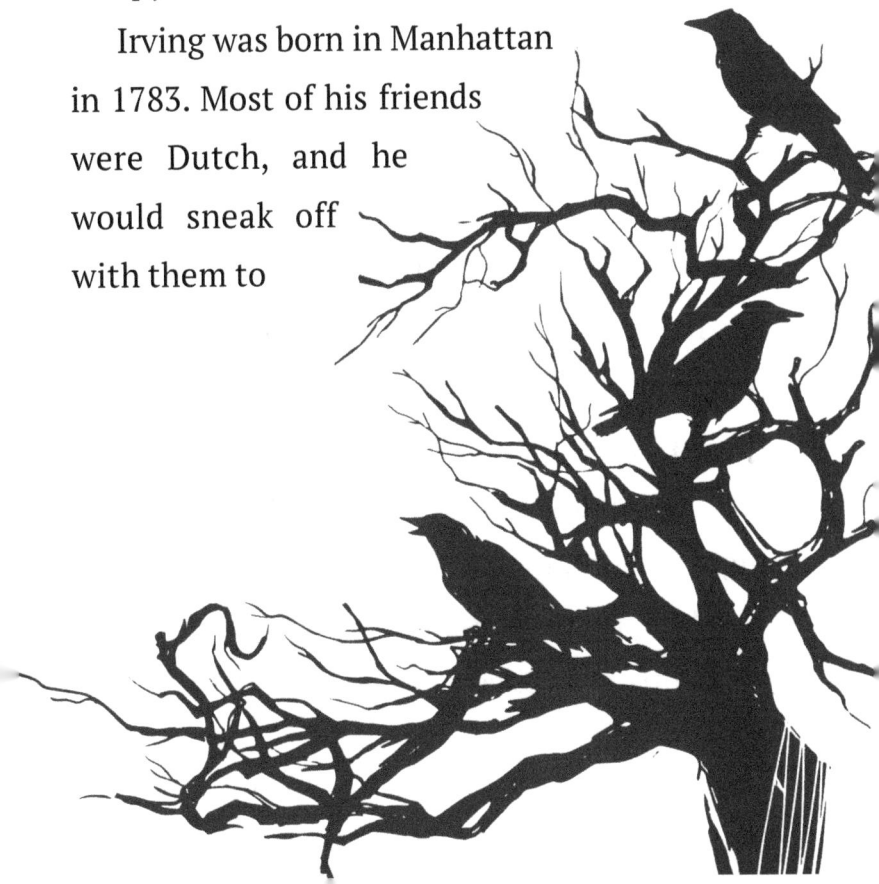

explore the lower Hudson Valley after his father said family prayers at night. They often hung out across the river in New Jersey, creating poems and getting into trouble by pulling pranks. The friends called themselves "the Lads of Kilkenny," and they would end up inspiring the prank to end all pranks in "The Legend of Sleepy Hollow."

At the time, nightwatchmen stood guard in little booths on certain corners of Manhattan. The booth was so small that it only left room to lean to the side and doze off, which many of the watchmen did. Most nights, nothing happened. But falling asleep on the job made the nightwatchmen the perfect target for boys looking to pull pranks in the middle of the night. One night, the Lads of Kilkenny found a watchman snoozing, so they tied a rope around his booth and yelled to wake him up. Before he knew what had happened, the Lads yanked the rope, sending the booth onto its side, guard inside. Then they dragged both through the cobblestone streets, laughing the entire time. It's quite possible the Lads inspired Brom Bones. A version of the nightwatchman prank is featured in "The Legend of Sleepy Hollow." But Brom wasn't the only character inspired by people from Irving's life.

In the cemetery at the Old Dutch Church, a particular tombstone stands out. Tourists searching for Katrina, Brom, and Ichabod in modern-day Sleepy Hollow often disturb the final resting place of a woman named Catriena Ecker van Tassel. Is this the real Katrina van Tassel? In reality,

Irving only borrowed the name. He created his Katrina van Tassel by mixing up things he liked about the Dutch American girls he met while traveling up and down the Hudson River. He admired their independence and spirit. By doing this, Irving made his story feel authentic without using real people in the pages. So, if the characters weren't actual people, does that mean he made everything else up too?

Yes and no. There's a lot more to explore on our journey through Sleepy Hollow's secrets.

You're probably saying to yourself, "Okay, but there's not actually a headless man running around, is there?"

Read on, traveler. We still have a long way to go.

Halloween in Sleepy Hollow

Who (or What) Was the Headless Horseman?

The very image of a headless figure charging about on a horse brings chills to even the bravest explorer in the world. So, is there any basis in the history of Sleepy Hollow for this infamous Horseman?

Many historians agree that Irving created his Horseman with a little help from someone you might have heard about: Aaron Burr. Our history books don't tell us much about Burr except that he killed Alexander Hamilton in a duel. If you like musicals, there's a pretty famous one you might have heard of that teaches all about Burr. But Burr was a friend of the Irving family, and they stood by him even after he became America's villain. He had been a soldier during the Revolutionary War and had a talent for telling stories. One of those stories captured Washington Irving's attention so much that it's believed to be the main inspiration for the Horseman. The story was about the Battle of White Plains, which occurred in White Plains, New York, on October 28, 1776.

What stuck out to Irving about the story Burr told was a journal entry made by General William Heath on October 31, 1776. The general saw a Hessian gunman lose his head.

An American cannon shot did the trick. It went on to say that the Americans also left one of the Hessian horses dead on the field. This combination has to be Irving's Headless Horseman and his ghostly horse, right? Not so fast!

This Halloween entry might not have been Irving's only inspiration for the Horseman's tale. We know that the Horseman throws a pumpkin at Ichabod Crane in the story. You might think that's because of this Halloween journal entry, and maybe it is, in part. But the more likely inspiration comes from something the Americans did on the battlefield at White Plains and other battles.

To make their cannon shots have a bigger impact, the soldiers heated the iron cannonballs and packed the cannons with material that would burn. So, when the cannonballs fired, they flew through the air like glowing pumpkins. They called them "hot shots."

Aaron Burr and Washington Irving heard many stories of the Revolutionary War at the best place in Sleepy Hollow for gossip: Van

Tassel's Tavern. The tavern stood along a major road, so locals and passersby stopped there. Irving and his friends came up from New York City often. Farmers, travelers, and trade workers made up a large part of the crowd, and many had fought in the war.

Stories flew around the tavern as the soldiers relived their memories of the war. Sometimes the stories were funny, and Irving and his friends would laugh along. But other times, the soldiers grew quiet and whispered their tales, as if afraid of the dead hearing them. They described the Hessians as more monsters than men, standing seven feet tall. They also whispered about a headless villain—assumed to be the Hessian soldier—walking around.

They had reason to be scared. A year after the Battle of White Plains, a soldier documented the state of the battlefield. He wrote about the horror of finding the bodies of Hessians still decaying out in the open. Armies usually carried their dead away from the battlefield, especially important leaders. So coming across those bodies one year later must have really upset the soldier.

Can you imagine how gross it must have been to see that? Or worse, to smell that? It's like your most disgusting zombie nightmare came to life, with bodies rotting away in the sun instead of underground. Since no one buried the Hessians, maybe they couldn't rest. Maybe they still haunt White Plains, hiding from visitors in the mist that rolls across the old battlefield. If you're brave enough, there's a small monument marking the site where the Hessians fell. It's called Merit Hill. A cannon on top of the monument is an eerie reminder of what happened. But if you want to chase the headless Hessian, fiction is the path you need to take.

"The Legend of Sleepy Hollow" mentions that the Headless Horseman was buried in

Sleepy Hollow at the Old Dutch Church, nine miles from White Plains. You might think Irving made it up, because why would the townspeople bury one of those monstrous soldiers in their town? But a headless Hessian is actually buried right where Irving says he is, as strange as that sounds. Even stranger, the van Tassel family that Washington Irving made famous made sure it happened.

After a tough defeat in the Revolution, British soldiers began taking land around New York City. They demanded the van Tassels surrender their farm, but the family fought back. Normally, the British would give families fifteen minutes to clear out of their homes and then burn them to the ground. At the van Tassel house, though, the Hessians had orders to move forward without waiting. They dragged the family members outside as they set fire to the house.

But not all of the family made it out. Elizabeth van Tassel screamed that two of her children remained. The older one managed to jump out of a window. Elizabeth tried to go into the house to get her sleeping baby, but the flames forced her back. Taking pity on Elizabeth, a Hessian went in and found the child, bringing her out wrapped in a quilt.

The family had no idea who this Hessian was and no way to thank him for his moment of kindness. But when people began to finally

clean up the bodies left at White Plains, the van Tassels got an idea. They thought burying the headless Hessian in an unmarked grave would honor the kindness shown to them by another. It was a nice thing to do, but little did they know that without his head, the Hessian could never truly rest.

Just like in "The Legend of Sleepy Hollow," people claim that this headless soldier rides through town on dark nights. The mist swirls in the air, and the veil between this world and the supernatural one feels thin. Many have reported hearing horse hooves at the current cemetery bridge. There have even been sightings of a ghostly form riding

over the old bridge nearby—a bridge that doesn't exist anymore.

Are you scared yet? If you're starting to wonder if maybe Sleepy Hollow really is haunted, just you wait, for this town has scarier tales to tell than a ghostly soldier looking for a head to take.

CHAPTER 6

A Cursed Land

Prior to the Revolution, war among local Native American tribes had left corpses unburied and scattered across a large open field like stones, adding a layer of supernatural energy around a particular Hokohongus tree—which is a giant chestnut tree—that had special meaning to the Native tribes, as you'll soon read.

Legend tells us that the local Weckquasgeek tribe felt disrespected by another tribe who came onto Weckquasgeek land without permission and without trading. This other tribe took whatever they wanted from the land but left nothing in its place. They also threatened war. The Weckquasgeek held a council meeting at a great stone near the Hokohongus tree. The chief demanded the tribe act. An elderly member known for having visions told the tribe they needed to curse the others for not making peace.

The curse they performed put the other tribe into a deathly sleep. The story goes that nature then turned their bones into stones,

which littered the open field. No one used the land. If they had, the spirits would have been disturbed. When the Dutch came to settle the area, the local tribes warned them of the curse, but the Dutch didn't listen. Instead, they prepared the land for planting, digging up the cursed stones. The ghosts of hundreds of Natives rose up, transferring some of the spell to the Dutch. Their spirits now mingle with those of the slain British and American troops who died on the battlefields nearby.

This fabled Hokohongus tree and its legend gives weight to the claims that Sleepy Hollow

puts both locals and visitors under its spell. Many tales have been told about several cursed spots in the area, and one of those is known as Balance Rock. The tribes believed that powerful storm spirits called Thunder Beings lived above the land in the clouds. This Algonquin myth helped the tribes explain thunder and lighting. If someone did something they shouldn't, the tribes told that the Thunder Beings might punish them. At Balance Rock, a medicine man accidentally fired a gun, and the Thunder Beings hit him with a bolt of lightning. You can still see the mark in the stone where the lighting went through him.

The ghosts of the tribes linger, as do the ghosts of colonists and soldiers. So much so that reports of sightings come from locals and tourists alike. When local high school students started an ambitious project to document

Sleepy Hollow's ghosts, they found evidence of repeated interactions with dozens of different ghosts. Some apartment buildings, built on top of the old Wiley's Swamp, crawl with ghosts of soldiers. Try to play golf at the course across from the cemetery, and you might hear a spirit cursing and blocking your perfectly lined-up putts. People have even spotted a Bigfoot-like creature in the woods who reportedly twisted hunting rifles around a tree.

The blood spilled in Sleepy Hollow seems to make it home to a high level of paranormal energy, whether we recognize it or not. Whatever the explanation, you can't help but wonder who or what walks with you when you visit.

Sleepy Hollow Lighthouse

Ghosts on the Water

Not all ghosts in the area come from the land. The Hudson River is also a magnet for the supernatural, mostly centered around one unique part of the river. There is a spot where the river widens to about three miles across, known as the Tappan Zee. "Zee" means "sea" in Dutch, and the name "Tappan Zee" brings together the Dutch and Algonquin languages, as well as the two peoples, all in one area.

Unfortunately, it was not a happy history. The Algonquin and Dutch cultures clashed. But a string of deadly robberies along the Tappan Zee in the early 1600s left both Native and European locals finally agreeing on something. They all felt the supernatural at work in the river. The waves beat harder than they should have against ships. The wind was unpredictable and moody, even on calm days, and the fog could become so thick at times, crossing the river would be too dangerous.

Both cultures had their own beliefs and superstitions about paranormal influence around the Tappan Zee. Natives believed river spirits caused the issues. Dutch sailors prayed to Saint Nicholas for protection. (Yes, that Saint Nicholas, also known as Santa! Did you know that in addition to bringing toys to good boys and girls, Sint Heer Klaas, as the Dutch

Americans knew him, offered protection when traveling over water?)

The unpredictable waters of the Hudson River, especially the Tappan Zee area, required sturdy boats. The Dutch designed a special boat called a sloop to get passengers and goods from New York City to Albany. The trip took as little as forty-eight hours by sloop. (The same trip today takes a little less than three hours by train.)

They designed sloops to hold lots of cargo but also have comfortable cabins for passengers wanting to make the trip. Many of the boats were seventy-five feet long. But the most important

thing about the sloops was they could handle all the harsh conditions on the river. You might think traveling up a river would be an easy trip, but not on the Hudson! In some places along the shore, the hills rise up to more than a thousand feet on each side, trapping the fierce and unpredictable wind. To deal with these conditions, sloops had flat, wide bottoms for support and low sides so if water came overboard, it wouldn't stay long and weigh down the boat.

The journey between New York City and Albany by sloop could be a dangerous one. The skippers who captained the boats had fourteen sections of river to go through before completing their journey. Each section had its own challenges, but the skippers and crews believed something more than just the wind affected the river. Many remembered a legend told on Germany's Rhine River of a beautiful siren, the Lorelei, who put ship captains under a spell and then wrecked the ships along the rocks.

Sirens show up in the stories of many other cultures, too. You may have read about sirens in Greek mythology or tales from different countries in Europe and the United Kingdom. They're similar to mermaids but much scarier. A mermaid might steal your shiny

gold watch or a ribbon out of your hair. But if sirens convinced sailors to move off course, those sailors were never seen again. It's not surprising that something similar became part of Hudson River lore, considering how common the legends are.

Sloop sailors believed something just as dangerous as the Lorelei prowled along the Hudson. Sailors told frightening tales of spirits called imps who looked for ships to mess with. History tells us that hundreds of deaths on the river were blamed on the imps.

So who or what are these imps? And how did sailors protect themselves? If imps could take down a whole sloop, what chance did any of the sailors have?

Imps were said to be the spirits of those who drowned in the Hudson River. They lived in the mists and came out of hiding to force ships to respect their leader, Dwerg. All captains wore hats when they sailed. So if you didn't tip your hat and show your respect, Dwerg, known as the "Heer of the Donder-Berg," would call his army of imps to get revenge. Dwerg used a trumpet to make his voice heard, calling across the river in Dutch.

But Dwerg and his imps weren't the only residents of the river. Mother Kronk, the witch of the Highlands, is said to be covered in fish scales, with two fish living in her eye sockets! Mother Kronk would shake her tablecloth to stir up a surprise storm and send lightning shooting out of her witches' pot on the fire. It is said she loved to boil her brew from the bones of the sloop skippers who never made it back to shore alive.

The imp army would then sink the ship by thunder, lightning, waves, and wind. Hundreds of sloops lie at the bottom of the deepest spot of the river, 218 feet down. It's known

to sailors as the "World's End." I don't know about you, but the name makes me want to avoid going there!

Imagine for a minute that you're a sailor on one of the sloops heading to Albany. It's your first time making the trip, and you've heard all the tales of the imps. You're so nervous that you feel like you're going to throw up, and each whistle of the wind reminds you of Dwerg's trumpet. What would you do if you saw an imp? And what do they even look like?

If you believe the legends, first they'll show up as

mist or maybe a little curl of fog. When you see that, you better shut your eyes tight, because if you open them, you might see the imp's true form: a petrified version of the human they used to be. That would be enough to give anyone nightmares for life!

You might think that the imps wouldn't bother modern-day sailors. But as with all things paranormal, time means nothing to them. Even in the twenty-first century, sailors aren't safe from the mischief of the imps— or worse.

Sit down with locals in Sleepy Hollow, and you'll hear how a real estate agent sailing with her husband had a strange experience near Donderberg Mountain just a few years ago. Patches of fog came up from the river. The wind pelted the boat from two different sides. Her husband did everything he was supposed to do, but the ship started going the wrong direction! When he tried to bring it back, the boat spun around. They had no control over their sails. The agent said it felt like they couldn't control the boat at all.

A schoolteacher had a similar experience several years ago. The fog rose, and a thunderstorm slammed into his motorboat in a flash. The river's shoreline disappeared into the mist, and he couldn't tell what direction he was headed. Just as he started to get scared, everything stopped. But not before the mysterious storm blew off his hat!

Now, Dwerg and his imp army may be the scariest spirits to haunt the Tappan Zee, but they aren't the only ones! Stay out too late on a Saturday night, and you just might meet the ghost of Rambout van Dam. Rambout made a promise he didn't honor, so the Tappan Zee punished him for it.

Before he set out for a Saturday night of fun, Rambout promised his minister he'd return before the church bell rang at midnight, which was the start of the Sabbath—a day of rest and religious observance. The promise Rambout made was a serious one.

Later that night, he jumped into his boat to head back down the river, but the currents blocked his oars. He had to work harder against the weight of the tide, and he soon disappeared into the rising mist. Maybe he knew what that meant, or maybe he didn't. But you know from our tales of ships on the Tappan Zee that the mist isn't what it seems. If it gets you, there's no hope for you.

As Rambout worked to move across the water, fingers of mist pulled at his boat. They kept it away from the shore. At midnight, the church bell rang, but Rambout still rowed, just as his ghost has been rowing ever since,

through the gloomy hours of early Sunday morning.

Today, his ghostly skeleton—dressed in rags—is said to row toward the shore but never make any progress. He's hard to see, as the mist surrounds him. But if you look closely, you might spot his eyes, burning green with jealousy.

Rambout's ghostly ship is not the only one out there. There's another ghostly ship that you may run across: the *Flying Dutchman*. You might have heard about the *Dutchman* in other tales. The ship's captain had to make a difficult journey, and he cursed both God and the Devil for having to do it.

The price he paid doomed himself and his crew to sail forever. But when a ghostly crew member finds love, his curse is broken. The men only have one night every seven years to make it happen. The rest of the time, they sail the world, unable to rest. Some unearthly force powers the *Flying Dutchman*. It never needs wind to fill its sails, and it travels in storms without issue. It's even made several appearances on the Tappan Zee over the years. During the Revolutionary War, the British army fired a cannon at it. The shot went straight through the rigging and the mast, which should have taken it down. But the ship vanished. A man in Sleepy Hollow later swore he'd escaped the *Dutchman* when a local woman fell in love with him. He said he'd made seven trips to land while on the *Dutchman* but was the only sailor on those trips to break the spell.

So if you sail the Tappan Zee, best to keep alert. Watch for the silent *Flying Dutchman* sailing by. Don't stay out past midnight on Saturday. And whatever you do, make sure you tip your hat to Dwerg! Only then will you be safe to carry on your way.

The Witch of Sleepy Hollow

The Old Dutch Church in Sleepy Hollow appears in many of the tales of the area, probably because it is a central place in town history. You already know that Washington Irving was inspired by it, and on one of his visits there, he learned of a fascinating character in local legend: Mother Hulda.

According to legend, Mother Hulda was a German witch doctor. Her cottage sat close to the bridge where Ichabod Crane tried and failed to escape the Headless Horseman. Washington Irving didn't directly mention Hulda in "The Legend of Sleepy Hollow," only a brief reference to a German witch doctor. But her presence in Sleepy Hollow cannot be denied.

Most of what we know about Mother Hulda comes from oral history, as not much had been written about her before the end of the 1800s. Was Mother Hulda an actual person who lived in Sleepy Hollow? Or a mashup of various legends brought from Europe? Let's do a little digging to find out.

Hulda's name has its origins in ancient Germany, although she was sometimes called "Holda" or "Holle." In fact, German ties to Hulda are so strong that in the German state of Hessen, Hulda's name is used to refer to snowfall. When it snows, they say that Hulda is shaking her blanket or that the town sleeps under Hulda's blanket. The Dutch also had a nature goddess named Hulda, so we can't rule out local Dutch farmers continuing a legend from their homeland, either.

In German tales, Hulda spent her time predicting the weather, spinning flax into cloth, and practicing witchcraft, which is why she was sometimes known as the "Dark Grandmother." There's a German fairy tale about Hulda taking in two local girls for a time. The one who was kind and helpful got to collect gold from Hulda to take home. The one who was greedy and refused to work went home covered in pitch—a thick, sticky goo

that comes out of trees. Some versions say that the pitch never really came off.

We do know that Sleepy Hollow's Mother Hulda settled in the area around 1770. This

strange old woman who lived alone reminded townspeople of all the superstitions from the Old World. She wore a flowing cloak, was thin with deep-set eyes, and had a Bohemian appearance. The people of Bohemia, now part of the Czech Republic, were considered untrustworthy by neighboring countries. The fear of their customs and culture also led to a lot of discrimination against them, and such was the case for Mother Hulda in Sleepy Hollow. At the time she arrived, country people in both Europe and America were suspicious of single women, even if they had been previously married. They viewed any widow over the age of fifty as a witch if she lived alone.

Giving women like Hulda the label of "witch" was a common thing in the Dutch colonies, and that label could be dangerous. The church branded witches as evil. Any woman could be accused of witchcraft with little to no proof. In fact, using herbs as medicine was commonly considered proof of witchcraft, but it was also a common practice at the time.

With their "proof" in hand, church officials would hold a trial to determine if a woman was guilty of being a witch. The trial was more like a play or movie than an actual trial to determine whether someone committed a crime. But witch trials had a very serious outcome: death. In many cases, a

woman convicted of being a witch was tied to a wood post and burned alive.

You've probably figured out by now that most women accused of being a witch were found guilty. This practice continued along the Hudson River until the early 1800s, with the last witch trial in New York happening in 1815, near Nyack. In fact, the Dutch colonists feared witches so much that they had all kinds of superstitions to ward them off. Their most popular protection involved nailing a horseshoe to their door. They believed the horseshoes brought good luck and protected the house so a witch could not enter or affect them with her magic.

But witch or not, outsiders weren't exactly welcome in Sleepy Hollow—ever. In fact, the minister of the Old Dutch Church ordered the townspeople to avoid talking to Mother Hulda, without knowing anything else about her. It didn't help Mother Hulda's case that her arrival made the town grow from twelve to *thirteen* families—an unlucky number indeed.

When Mother Hulda showed up at the local store for the first time, no one would speak to her. Nobody knew where she lived until one day, a farmer found her hut while he was looking for his lost cow. It was off the beaten path, in an area thought to be cursed by Native American tribes. Why would someone live there? The townspeople thought there must be something wrong with Mother Hulda to live there. The farmer also found lots of dried herbs around her hut. Mother Hulda was going to use them for medicines, but you know what the townspeople thought, right? Right. Witchcraft.

Hulda spoke in a tribal dialect the farmer could not understand. He asked a local man from the Weckquasgeek tribe to speak with Hulda. She said she had only come to live nearby and barter baskets, furs, and medicines. Many of the nearby tribes had died out, and the Weckquasgeek man thought she might have been a widow or a captive of one of those tribes who had nowhere to go.

You might wonder why the town didn't have more sympathy for Hulda. After all, the translator said she might have been a captive of one of the tribes. But that was exactly the problem for them. The fact that a white woman spoke a tribal language

and had spent time in their community meant to the Dutch colonists that she'd chosen the Native American people over her own people. They didn't view her as one of their own. It wouldn't have mattered even if she'd been taken as a child. It was wrong judge Hulda, but fear and superstition fueled the townspeople's' animosity toward her.

Of course, that didn't stop many of them from taking advantage of her talents, trading with her for handmade baskets and warm furs. But they wouldn't talk to her. Even kind people who didn't agree with the harsh views of the rest of the town feared the minister and going against God, so they didn't talk to her either.

The most vocal anti-Hulda townspeople did accept that their neighbors traded furs and baskets with her, but medicine was different to them because of the ties to witchcraft. In public, people loudly told everyone they took no medicine from her. But bundles of herbs showed up outside their doors when anyone in the house became sick, and they used them. They knew where the medicine had come from and privately thanked Hulda with valuable items like sewing needles, lamps, and cooking pots.

Finally, though, people's opinion of Mother Hulda began to shift during the Revolutionary War. The fighting tore apart the area, with each side controlling half of the county, leaving Sleepy Hollow in a neutral zone in the middle. Both sides had groups who would raid the area, taking whatever they wanted from the farms. The British raiders were called the "Cowboys," and the American raiders were called the "Skinners." Mother Hulda brought victims of the raids medicinal plants as well as things like dried meat, vegetables, and even maple syrup sweets.

One day while Hulda was out gathering medicine, the British landed warships in the Tappan Zee. The militiamen in Sleepy Hollow didn't have many weapons and weren't well-trained, so they feared going against the heavily armed British. But Hulda wasn't afraid. She grabbed her musket and stood right on the front line. Hulda was a sharpshooter, and the British sent dragoons—soldiers on horseback—to stop her. Instead, she drew them away from Sleepy Hollow, getting them lost in the process.

When the rest of the British retreated, everyone looked for their heroine. They found her lifeless body a short distance from the Old Dutch Church, taken down by a ball of lead from a musket. They didn't know what to do. Many feared touching her in case she could harm them, still fearful of what they didn't understand, despite all of her kindness. But others insisted on a burial for Mother Hulda.

A search of her hut revealed a Bible and a will leaving her gold to war widows for their care. That convinced the townspeople that she deserved to be honored with a proper burial. Even the reverend came around to Hulda, agreeing to an unmarked grave by the north wall of the Old Dutch Church. For someone buried in an unmarked grave, Mother Hulda certainly left a mark on Sleepy Hollow. Many visitors to the area ask about her, and in 2019, she finally got the recognition she deserved. She now has a headstone to mark her grave as "Hulda of Bohemia. Healer. Herbalist. Patriot."

So seek out her grave if you ever make it to Sleepy Hollow. Leave her a flower or two. I think she'd like that. And if you happen to run into her ghost, don't be scared. She keeps to herself, and she might just be protecting you from something lurking in the shadows!

The Women in White

Apparitions know as the "Women in White" pop up in many cultures, especially in American urban legend. Some legends consider them powerful fairies. Others give the label to women who died too soon, often under violent circumstances. Washington Irving only gives a quick mention of a woman in white in "The Legend of Sleepy Hollow": the one who haunts Raven Rock. But the Raven Rock woman in white isn't the only one in the area. She's also not the only one who screams just before a storm. Like Mother Hulda, the Women in White of Sleepy Hollow seem more concerned with protecting than haunting.

Raven Rock's geography makes it a prime spot for spooky tales. A jagged, thirty-foot ledge overlooks the isolated area, and legend speaks of a woman's voice that can be heard, warning of winter storms. Locals swear, even today, that a woman's spirit lingers deep within the region. She can be tracked floating across the cemetery toward the river, warning of bad weather with unearthly moans. But some say the strongest screams come from someone else: a heartbroken woman who died during the Revolutionary War, high above the Hudson River.

Imagine you lived near the Hudson River in the late 1700s. Your life would be very different, for obvious reasons: no computers, no lights, and no electricity, to mention a few things. But the thing you'd need most—especially in winter—was heat. And without firewood to burn, there'd be no heat.

One afternoon, a poor farm wife sensed a snowstorm coming but knew she didn't have enough wood to last. The cottage already felt bitterly cold, so she bundled up in thick wool and went in search of her prize. The minister at the Old Dutch Church suggested she look near Raven Rock, as some good branches had fallen when the farmers cut trees to clear the land.

Along the way, she scooped up some chestnut and pine wood. As she passed Mother Hulda's cottage, she left some of the wood as a thank you. Hulda had given her medicine a few days earlier. Hulda didn't host visitors often, but that day, she tried to convince the farm wife to come in for tea. She warned of the coming storm, but the farmer's wife said she'd be fine.

Soon, though, the snow started, and the trail and trees blended together. Raven

Rock loomed over the farmer's wife, and she crouched down in its protection, hoping the snow would stop falling for a few minutes. But the snow didn't let up. Instead, it blanketed everything, including her. The space around her took on a dreamy, enchanted feeling, and she had to fight to stay awake. The cold seeped through her thick wool wrap and settled into her bones. She didn't have the strength to make her way home. With no energy and no hope of getting home, she fell asleep and never woke up.

The townspeople buried her in the cemetery of the Old Dutch Church. But her spirit isn't at rest. When snowstorms approach and the wind stirs up the leaves, her voice carries across the mist. She doesn't want to scare you with her cries, but in her mind, that's better than the alternative. Her wails are a painful warning of what can happen if you venture out in the storm, and you'd do well to listen.

Sleepy Hollow's other lady in white has a very different tale to tell, but it's just as heartbreaking.

You already know that during the Revolutionary War, the rebel colonists fought the British. King George III had tried to keep strict rule over the colonies, but it didn't work. A lot of the colonists wanted freedom from him and his laws. They wanted to make their own decisions and stop paying his outrageous taxes. The king wanted loyalty, so every act of rebellion from the colonists made him hit back hard with stricter laws and penalties. You can see why things ended up in war.

During the war, British soldiers occupied much of the colonies. Most colonists feared the British soldiers. They were afraid to show support of the rebel colonists. So when the king's soldiers demanded food and rest in their homes, the colonists couldn't say no. If they did, the consequence could be death.

Do you remember reading about the Battle of White Plains earlier? Well, after the battle, many of the British officers looked for homes along the Hudson River while they waited for orders from their generals. Several made their way to Sleepy Hollow, including a handsome young lieutenant and the officer above him.

The men opened the door of a small cottage where a fire crackled in the fireplace. They found a shy woman, believed to be named Gertje, hiding behind a flour barrel. Gertje had heard stories about other homes in the area that had been burned by the Hessians. Her brothers fought on different sides of the war, so the home was all she had. She hoped the British soldiers would see how simply she lived and look elsewhere. But fate had other plans.

Turned out, the lieutenant and Gertje got along right away. He treated her with kindness and made her feel more comfortable, even when his superior officer was rude and demanding. Their commander delayed sending orders, so the lieutenant and Gertje had a lot of time to get to know each other.

Townspeople warned Gertje she should stay away from the lieutenant. He was a British soldier, so they said the relationship had no future and he'd leave. They warned she might be accused of being a spy or get caught in between the two armies somehow. But Gertje had already fallen in love.

When his orders came, the lieutenant took her to Raven Rock, high above the town, to ask her to marry him. He had two months left in the king's army, and he promised to return for her. He planned to sail through the Tappan Zee to Sleepy Hollow to meet her, and then they'd head to his family's sugar plantation in Jamaica to live their lives together. He told her to look from Raven Rock for the white topsail of his ship.

While her love fought George Washington and the rebels, Gertje pulled scraps of white fabric together and created a patchwork wedding dress. She again ignored all warnings from the townspeople, insisting it was true love.

Exactly two months later, Gertje put on her wedding gown and went up to Raven Rock. She looked out across the Tappan Zee, searching for her love's ship. Instead, she found the first winter storm. Steely clouds rolled in. The river churned, and the winds pierced through the fabric of her dress. She called out to her soldier, but only the harsh winds answered. Her voice grew hoarse. Frostbite consumed her hands and cheeks and her lips blistered.

She feared her soldier had died on a battlefield in New Jersey, but rumor has it that the superior officer locked the soldier up, knowing of his plans to return to Gertje. Better that than the embarrassment of a British soldier running away with a colonial girl. Gertje didn't return home, and no one saw her after the storm. They all thought she ran away to New York City, upset that her soldier hadn't returned. But eventually, everyone learned the truth. Two huntsmen searching for rabbit on Raven Rock found more than they wanted to. Gertje's frozen body lay trapped under the ice and snow. They ran to the Old Dutch Church to get the minister and asked him to bring his Bible. He recognized Gertje immediately. Like the farmer's wife, Gertje was buried at the Old

Dutch Church, but her spirit remains restless. When the weather turns, she takes her place on the cliffs looking out over Sleepy Hollow. Her cries to her love have become a warning.

The Line Between Reality and Fantasy

Who can say what is actually real or not in Sleepy Hollow? The inspiration for the legends certainly feel real, and a lot of facts stand behind the stories. And the fear behind them is definitely real. The thrill of exploring it all never goes away for those like you and me who love dark and mysterious tales of things you cannot explain.

If you visit Sleepy Hollow, why not make it a point to listen for the Women in White of Raven Rock? Be sure to tip your hat in the direction of Donderberg Mountains and check in on Mother Hulda—maybe you'll find she left a bundle of herbs for you.

Don't forget to also search for Washington Irving's ghost in the place he loved so much. The classic story he brought us still has meaning, after all this time. It certainly changed the course of history for Sleepy Hollow, New York.

He also probably knew a lot more about the Horseman and the otherworld of Sleepy Hollow than he let on. He wrote once that he believed he'd haunt Sunnyside, his home in Sleepy Hollow, once he died. But he comforted readers not to be afraid because he'd be a good spirit.

Try to picture him now, standing at the Old Dutch Church, making sure the ghosts of Sleepy Hollow stay in line. Smiling at the sound of horse hooves on the bridge and warnings in the air. Maybe one day, you'll even get to meet him. Until then, keep chasing Ichabod and watch out for flying pumpkins!

Jessa Dean writes spooky stories for kids and has been a ghostwriter for multiple authors who unfortunately don't write about ghosts. She lives in Houston with feline overlords who like to "help" with her work. Her day job in law proves truth is stranger than fiction.

Check out some of the other Spooky America titles available now!

Original *Legends and Lore of Sleepy Hollow and the Hudson Valley* author Jonathan Kruk is a master storyteller! Every year, he performs for thousands of children at hundreds of schools, libraries and historic sites in the Hudson Valley and metropolitan New York. His work has been featured on the Travel and History Channels. Here's more from Jonathan Kruk:

www.jonathankruk.com